OTHER BOOKS BY IYANLA VANZANT

*Living Through the Meantime*
*Until Today!*
*Yesterday, I Cried*
*Don't Give It Away!*
*In the Meantime*
*One Day My Soul Just Opened Up*
*Faith in the Valley*
*The Value in the Valley*
*Acts of Faith*

# Every Day I Pray

Prayers for Awakening to the

Grace of Inner Communion

## Iyanla Vanzant

PHOTOGRAPHS BY CHRISTINA LESSA

SIMON & SCHUSTER

NEW YORK   LONDON   TORONTO   SYDNEY   SINGAPORE

SIMON & SCHUSTER
Rockefeller Center
1230 Avenue of the Americas
New York, NY 10020

*Simon & Schuster* and colophon are registered trademarks
of Simon & Schuster, Inc.

Designed by Jeanette Olender
Photo illustrations by Christina Lessa
Manufactured in the United States of America

1   3   5   7   9   10   8   6   4   2

Library of Congress Cataloging-in-Publication Data is available.

ISBN 0-684-86000-7

For information regarding special discounts for bulk purchases,
please contact Simon & Schuster Special Sales at 1-800-456-6798
or business@simonandschuster.com

This book is dedicated

to the memory of my sister

Her Royal Highness Leola Iyalu Oredola Opeodu

and to my stepmother and best friend,

Lynnette May Brown Harris

## ACKNOWLEDGMENTS

I would like to acknowledge my prayer partners and supporters, those who have consistently reminded me to pray and engaged in many hours of prayer with me or for me:

Rev. Shaheerah Stephens, Rev. Raina Bundy, Rev. Barbara King, Rev. Helen Carey, Rev. Johnnie Coleman, Rev. Michael Beckwith, Rev. Linda Hollies, Rev. Roger Teel, Rev. Mary Mann Morrisey, Rev. Jeremiah Wright, Sarah Porter, Vivian Berryhill, Rev. Chester Berryhill, Wilhelmina Myrie, Elvia Myrie, Ken and Rene Kizer, Norman L. Frye, Bernadette Griggs; my sacred sisters Hilda Boulware, Cheryl McDowell, Jennifer Sackett and Libby Dubin; Stanley and Chemin Bernard, Drs. Ron and Mary Hulnick, Drs. Gay and Kathlyn Hendricks, Dr. Na'im Akbar, Suzie Ormond, the Inner Visions Worldwide faculty and staff, the class of 2001 of the University of Santa Monica and all of those whose names I do not know.

In bringing this book to life I would like to express my deepest gratitude to my editor, Trish Todd, whose patience and support is truly an answer to a prayer; my photographer, Christina Lessa, and her assistant, Dan Petrucelli; Zully Zurheide; my children Damon, Alex, Gemmia and Nisa, who continually give me things to pray about; my grandchildren Ashole, Oluwa, Niamoja, Adesola and David, who shaped my prayers into songs of thanksgiving; my husband, Adeyemi Bandele, and my very dear friend Marjorie Battle, whose presence in my life is evidence that *things go better with prayer.*

# CONTENTS

# INTRODUCTION

I grew up in the Holiness Church, where *prayer was an event*. On Sunday mornings, for as far back as I can remember, I watched one minister or another lead prayer. He always started out slowly, standing erect, his eyes closed and head bowed. Gradually the tempo changed. The pastor would take off his glasses and reach for the handkerchief in his pocket. Just about then, the organist would begin to play deep chords to accent certain words. This prompted the human chorus of humming, clapping, stomping and sometimes moaning. The pastor would start to sweat as the cadence of his speech changed. He was sort of singing, sort of talking. The organist kept pace with more chords, now accompanied by drums and an occasional tambourine. Soon most of the people in the church were on their feet, talking back to the pastor, helping him out with *"Amens"* and *"Glory Fathers,"* being driven to a feverish pitch by the *"Thank-Yous"* and *"Hallelujahs"* being shouted out from every corner of the sanctuary.

Prayer in the Holiness Church was an amazing, sometimes frightening, event for a child to witness. The energy that was revved up from the sanctuary certainly amazed me and made a lasting impression. Although I could barely understand a word the pastor was saying over the organ and the human orchestra, I knew something powerful was taking place. Sometimes I clapped because everyone else was clapping. Other times I clapped because I was afraid not to. I was afraid that if I did not clap, if I just sat there watching, God would think I didn't love him. God would think I didn't know how to pray to him. The conclusion I came away with was that I didn't know how to pray at all. Many years after I left the church that conclusion was still fresh in my mind. Sure, I knew all of the childhood prayers I uttered on my knees at the side of my bed. Many years of Sunday-school attendance had etched certain Psalms and rote prayers into the fibers of my brain. However, somewhere deep inside of me, I had the secret belief that I did not know how to pray, and that frightened me.

I'm not sure where I heard it or why I believed it, but when I was in my mid-twenties a few words changed my approach to and experience of prayer. The words were these: "Every thought you think is a prayer. Every word you speak is a prayer. Every act in which you engage is a prayer, because the Spirit of God lives in you." Now, how awesome is that? I didn't need drums. I didn't need to clap. I didn't need a host of other people to help me raise the volume of my prayers so that God would hear them. If the words of that statement are true, and I do believe they are, it means that at every moment of every day, I am communicating with the Creator of the universe. While this is not the prayer of the Holiness Church, I still find prayer to be both amazing and frightening. It is amazing because it means that God knows me from the inside out. It is frightening because some of my thoughts, words and actions are not things I would want to lay in God's lap for sanctioning. I realize that if God were to in fact put the power of his/her presence on some of the things that have been in my mind, I would be a hazard to myself. Thank God for divine wisdom, and thank God for grace.

Once I got it straight, I realized that the essence, energy, power and presence of God is in fact housed at the core of my being. I also understood that God does in fact hear my every thought and word. His/her response shows up as my experiences, my feelings and the many divine inspirations that have shaped the course of my life. I do believe that prayer is an inner communion with the divine. This means that when I am consciously participating in the communion amazing things can, will and do happen. In fact, they happen all of the time. However, my first challenge was learning to remain consciously involved in what I was thinking and saying so that I could be actively engaged in the process of communing with my Creator. This engagement would also help me to recognize the answer to the prayer when it showed up.

Scripture tells us to "Pray without ceasing," to honor

God in all of our ways so that s/he can direct our paths. In essence I have learned that I must talk to God, commune with God, stay conscious of God's presence within me at all times. It is through this understanding and desire that I have grown to love prayer. I sometimes jokingly say that I pray about everything, including what to wear and what to eat. In some ways the joke is very true. My thoughts are consistently focused on what I believe will bring honor to the presence of the divine within me. At times I have long conversations with God. Sometimes I ask questions. I admit that there are also times when I let out my frustrations, fears and anxieties in less than honorable ways. No matter what I pray about or how I pray about it, the result I always get is comfort. I find peace through prayer. Most important of all, I believe that I strengthen my connection to the almighty presence.

Over the years, I have received hundreds of letters from people who believe, as I once did, that they do not know how to pray. They are seeking a formula. They are afraid not to pray and even more afraid not to *pray right.* Remember: *every* thought, *every* word, *every* action *is a prayer.* If we can remain mindful of that, focusing our attention on honoring God's presence in everything and everyone, prayer will become as natural as breathing. If we can surrender, *give up the need* to do it right, by focusing on just doing it earnestly, honestly and with faith, our thoughts and words will be filled with God's radiant essence. When we slip, when we forget to be honorable or faithful, grace steps in. She translates the words to find the deeper meaning. Along with her sisters faith and hope, grace shapes our thoughts and words so that we get exactly what we need, a response to our prayer that will help us grow inwardly.

This book is a collection of prayers I have written over the years. I have found that writing a prayer helps to anchor it in my mind. Consequently, I have kept a Prayer Journal. Some of the prayers are based on or inspired by Scripture, others are just my thoughts, my intimate conversations with God. The prayers offered in this book cover a variety of topics and needs. It is my prayer that when you read them, they will spark a light within your heart. Perhaps in the presence of the light you will be inspired to write a prayer or two of your own. Or perhaps in reading them aloud, with your family or friends, you too will come to know and experience the peace of God's grace. I believe that words have the power to shape experiences and circumstances. Whether you are new to the premise and practice of prayer, or are already a "prayer warrior," I ask that you join with me in making the thoughts, words and actions of our everyday lives more reverent, honorable and loving. In this way, I believe that we will anchor the presence of peace, joy, balance, harmony and God on the planet. Toward that vision and intention I remain prayerfully purposed and poised.

Be blessed!

*Iyanla*

# Every Day I Pray

## For Building a Prayer Life

Dear God:

I thank you for the privilege of prayer.

I am aware that prayer is my direct line of communication to you.

I acknowledge that I can do more through prayer than I can do with my limited power.

I am so grateful that in my darkest hour, or my weakest moment, I can come to you in prayer.

I am so grateful that when the hopelessness of despair threatens to overtake me, I can come to you in prayer.

I thank you for the privilege of prayer.

I am so grateful that when my abilities and knowledge are inadequate to meet the challenges of my life, I can come to you in prayer.

I am so grateful that when I feel weak and helpless, I can come to you in prayer.

I am so grateful that when my family and friends turn
their backs in my times of need, or are not there to
encourage and support me, I can come to you in
prayer.

I thank you for the privilege of prayer.

I am so grateful that when I "can't," you can and you
do when I come to you in prayer.

I am so grateful that when I don't know, you *know,* and
you shower me with understanding and direction
when I come to you in prayer.

I am so grateful that when I don't know what to say or
what to do, you provide me with divine direction
and the power to speak the truth without hesitation,
if I simply come to you in prayer.

I thank you for the privilege of prayer.

I am so grateful that you are my mediator in the face of
strife and that you protect me from inner and outer
adversaries when I come to you in prayer.

I am so grateful that you are my supporter, my cheer-
leader, my strongest advocate.

You inspire me, motivate me and help me to take

the most appropriate steps when I come to you in
   prayer.

I thank you for the privilege of prayer.

I am so grateful that no matter what the situation may
   be, no matter how I am feeling or what I am doing, I
   can come to you at any time, under all circumstances, in prayer.

I am so grateful that there is nothing that you and I
   can't do together when I bring you any concern or
   request in prayer.

I thank you for the privilege of prayer, for your swift
   response to every prayer I offer.

Thank you, God, for hearing my prayer.

Thank you for receiving my prayer.

Thank you, God, for the awesome power and privilege
   of prayer.

For all I have received and all that is yet to come, I
   humbly offer my prayer of gratitude.

And So It Is!

*(After reciting this prayer, spend five to ten minutes in silence.)*

## Morning Prayer

Dear God:

This is the day that you have made, and I am so grateful to be a part of it.

This is a day unlike any other day, and I am so grateful for this opportunity to begin again. This is the day I will place myself totally in your care.

This is the day that I will use to serve you in faith and joy. This is the day all of my spiritual and karmic debts are canceled, and I am so grateful to be free.

On this day, I now declare that I am free of fear! Free of doubt! Free of anger! Free of shame! Free of guilt! Free of unproductive thoughts and actions!

On this glorious day that you have allowed me to see, I am divinely determined and dutifully dedicated to live the life you have created for me.

*This is the day, God!*

*Your day! My day!*

A life of peace, joy, fulfillment, abundance and creative
   activity.
This is the day, God!
Your day! My day!
And for this day I am so very, very grateful.
And So It Is!

# Let There Be Light

Dear God:

Let there be light!

You, Lord, are my light!

Let there be joy!

You, Lord, are my joy!

Let there be peace!

You, Lord, are my peace!

Let there be an abundance of good things, right
  relationships and positive experiences in my life.

You, Lord, are my source of every good thing I need or
  desire!

Let my mind be filled with the wisdom of your
  presence.

You, Lord, are the infinite intelligence of the universe.
  You are my wisdom. You are the presence guiding

me to right thought, right action and the right
response in every experience.

Let my heart be filled with love, respect and honor for
myself and all other people.

You, Lord, are the presence of love, re-creating and
duplicating yourself at the core of my very being!

Let my body be filled with the radiant health and
wellness that comes with your presence.

Let my life be filled with the goodness, the peace, the
joy and the light of your divine radiance.

That is good! That is God!

Thank you, God!

Thank you, God!

Thank you, God, that before I ask, you have already
answered!

For my awareness of this as the reality of my being and
in my life, I am so grateful.

Let it be so!

And So It Is!

## Prayer of Acknowledgment

Dear God:

I acknowledge that you, God, are awesome!

I acknowledge that you, God, are magnificent!

I acknowledge that you, God, are amazing!

I acknowledge that you, God, are ever ready,
everywhere, to provide and protect.

I acknowledge that you, God, are a powerful presence
in every situation.

I acknowledge that you, God, are a skilled negotiator.

I acknowledge that you, God, are a peaceful mediator.

I acknowledge that you, God, are the master strategist.

I acknowledge that you, God, provide the way into all
things good and the way out of all things harmful.

I acknowledge your love!

I acknowledge your wisdom!

I acknowledge your compassion!

I acknowledge your mercy!

I acknowledge that you, God, are the solution to the problem.

I acknowledge that you, God, are the answer to the question.

I acknowledge that you, God, are the calm in the midst of turmoil.

My dear God, I acknowledge the power of your presence in my heart.

I acknowledge the power of your presence in my mind.

I acknowledge the power of your presence in my life.

I now stand bravely, boldly, calmly, powerfully filled with the magnificent, awesome, amazing strength of God.

I know that all is well with my soul and in my life. For this I am so grateful.

Let it be so!

And So It Is!

## Prayer for Alignment with God

*There is nothing to be healed, only God to be revealed.*
I now ask that the peace of God be revealed in my
   mind.
*There is nothing to be healed, only God to be revealed.*
I now ask that the love of God be revealed in my heart.
*There is nothing to be healed, only God to be revealed.*
I now ask that the perfection of God be revealed as my
   health.
*There is nothing to be healed, only God to be revealed.*
I now ask that the abundance of God be revealed as my
   wealth.
*There is nothing to be healed, only God to be revealed.*
I now ask that the presence of God be revealed as my
   joy.

*There is nothing to be healed, only God to be revealed.*

I now ask that the power of God be revealed as protection for me and my family.

*There is nothing to be healed, only God to be revealed.*

Thank you, God, for revealing yourself as peace in my life.

Thank you, God, for revealing yourself as love in my life.

Thank you, God, for revealing yourself as the joy of my life.

Thank you, God, for revealing yourself at the center of my life.

Thank you, God, for defending me, protecting me, guiding me, taking care of everything that concerns me and enabling me to do everything that I am asked to do.

Thank you, God, for healing my relationships and my body.

Thank you, God, for providing my every need.

Most of all, God, I thank you for loving me just as I

am, for knowing what I need and for being the
fulfillment of my needs, even before I ask.
Today, I acknowledge, I accept, I believe there is
nothing that needs to be fixed, changed or healed,
because God, my God, will always be revealed.
For this I am so grateful.
And So It Is!

## Practicing the Presence of God

I am immersed in the sacred presence of God.
From the depths of my soul, my prayers rise up on
wings of faith and flow out into the universe.
What a joy it is to know that when I pray I am
heard.
And when my prayers are heard, they are answered.
In stressful times I will remember that there is an
absolute calm in the midst of the storm.
This calm is the sacred presence of God.
It is there I want to be.
I now let my thoughts move toward God, knowing
that God hears all, knows all and gives all.
For this I am so very grateful.
And So It Is!

*I am immersed in the sacred*

*presence of God.*

## Welcoming the Holy Spirit
### into Your Life

Holy Spirit, you are welcome in my mind.
Holy Spirit, you are welcome in my mind.
Holy Spirit, you are welcome in my mind.
Transform my mind, Holy Spirit.
Bring my every thought into alignment with God's
   perfect plan for my life.

Holy Spirit, you are welcome in my heart.
Holy Spirit, you are welcome in my heart.
Holy Spirit, you are welcome in my heart.
Transform my heart, Holy Spirit.
Erase every feeling, memory and experience that is not
   a reflection of God's love for me.

· · ·

Holy Spirit, you are welcome in my life.
Holy Spirit, you are welcome in my life.
Holy Spirit, you are welcome in my life.
Transform every condition, situation and circumstance
   of my life. Make my life a living reflection of the
   goodness and glory of God.

Holy Spirit, transform me, transform me, transform
   me.
Transform every part of me that is not in keeping with
   God's love, God's goodness, God's purpose and God's
   perfect plan for me to live a life of joy, peace,
   wholeness, ease, harmony and abundance.

Holy Spirit, you are welcome in my mind.
Holy Spirit, you are welcome in my heart.
Holy Spirit, you are welcome in my life.
Help me to be all that God created me to be.
For your presence I am so grateful.
Let it be so!
And So It Is!

## Prayer for Guidance

Dear God:

Please purge my agenda today. Take out of my life everything and everyone that could possibly take my focus from you. Take out of my mind every thought, every belief, every intention, every motivation that does not make you the priority in my life. Take out of my heart every experience, every memory, every desire that does not serve your purpose for my life. Remind me that your plan, your love for me is my salvation. Everything else is a figment of my imagination and a function of fear. Today, dear God, I recognize that I don't even know what to pray for, so I will leave the blessing up to you.

And So It Is!

## I Am!

I *Am* renewed, authorized and cleansed by the
authority of the Holy Spirit within me.

My steps are ordered, guided and blessed.

I *Am* a worthy vessel.

I *Am* a willing vessel.

I have been shaped and modeled by God's love.

I *Am* available for God's love to be accomplished
as me.

I *Am* equipped with the skill, the knowledge and the
ability to carry out the life assignments that God
has given to me with love.

I now go forth peacefully, joyfully and lovingly.

I *Am* bestowed with an abundance of good things
in all of my affairs and in every aspect of my
world.

I now go forth with the blessed assurance that I shall
never again forget that it is the Spirit of the
Father/Mother of life that has anointed me.
For this I am so grateful.
And So It Is!

## Prayer for Clarity

Dear Father God, Mother God, Blessed Holy Spirit:

Teach me to monitor my thoughts and desires to ensure that they are filled with love, harmony and peace for myself and everyone in my life, in all situations and under all circumstances.

Remind me that my mind can make loving, peaceful decisions and choices because you are a part of my mind.

I am willing and ready to enter a new life, a fearless life, a joy-filled life, a peaceful life.

I know that once I rid my mind of dark, doubtful, fearful thoughts, I will live the life I desire.

I believe that once my desire is centered on your love, your peace, your will, the reality I live will be the life I dream of.

Teach me, dear God, to change my thought patterns and to use my mind in an orderly way.

I now accept as truth that once I put my mind to proper use, I am renewed! I am invigorated! I am filled with the confidence of one who knows, feels and lives through the bounty of God's love, God's grace and God's unlimited, abundant good.

Let it be so!

And So It Is!

*A new life,*

*a fearless life.*

## I Am Willing to Change

*I Am* willing to change!

*I Am* willing to change my mind!

*I Am* willing to change my heart!

*I Am* willing to change the perception of myself and
the world around me!

*I Am* willing to change what I do and how I do it!

*I Am* willing to know change, to be changed and see
the miraculous change that change brings!

I know that I of myself can do nothing.

Therefore *I Am* willing to allow the Holy Spirit to heal
and change me at the soul level, that I may be all
that God created me to be.

*I Am* willing to be transformed, to have my true mind
restored, to have my heart renewed, according to
God's perfect plan.

And So It Is!

## Prayer of Transformation

I now consciously and willingly call forth the Holy Spirit and the consciousness of the *Higher Mind I Am* into every atom, every molecule, every cell, every tissue, every organ, every muscle, every living system in my being, asking to have transformed every energy, every pattern, every belief, every program, every idea, every attitude, every perception, every expectation, every intention and every motivation, every behavior, bringing all into alignment with the perfect will of God.

I now consciously and willingly call forth the Holy Spirit and the consciousness of the *Higher Mind I Am* into every atom, every molecule, every cell, every tissue, every organ, every muscle and every living system in my being, asking to have transformed every energy, every pattern, every belief, every program, every idea, every attitude, every perception, every expectation, every intention and every motivation, every behavior, bringing all into alignment with the perfect peace of God.

I now consciously and willingly call forth the Holy Spirit and the consciousness of the *Higher Mind I Am* into every atom, every molecule, every cell, every tissue, every organ, every muscle and every living system in my being, asking to have transformed every energy, every pattern, every belief, every program, every idea, every attitude, every perception, every expectation, every intention and every motivation, every behavior, bringing all into alignment with the perfect love of God.

For this I am so grateful.

And So It Is!

## Prayer for Inner Strength

Blessed Holy Spirit:

I was glad when you said to me, *"Let us go into the house of the Lord!"*

When my heart was heavy with grief, I went into the house of the Lord.

When my mind was overwhelmed with confusion, I went into the house of the Lord.

When my body was racked with pain, I went into the house of the Lord.

When my wallet and bank account were empty, I went into the house of the Lord.

When those who are nearest to me betrayed and despised me, I went into the house of the Lord.

When my greatest efforts were not recognized or rewarded, I went into the house of the Lord.

When I felt lost and unable to find my way, I went into
    the house of the Lord.

Thank you, God, that there is such a place *within* me
    and *for* me.

In your house there is peace of mind.

In your house there is safety.

In your house there is wholeness.

In your house there is clear direction.

In your house there is healing.

In your house there is unconditional love.

In your house there is inspiration.

In your house there is relief and release.

In your house there is compassion.

In your house there is joy.

In your house there is forgiveness.

In your house there is strength.

In your house there is power.

I was glad when you said to me, *"Let us go into the
    house of the Lord!"*

Thank you, God, for the standing invitation to come

into your house, for in your house my soul and my
mind find rest.
For this I am so grateful.
And So It Is!

## Please Untie the Nots

Dear God:

Please untie the *nots* that are invading my mind, my
heart and my life.

Please remove the have *nots,* the can *nots* and the do
*nots* that invade my mind.

Please erase the will *nots,* may *nots,* might *nots* that
invade my heart.

Please release me from the could *nots,* would *nots* and
should *nots* that invade my life.

Most of all, dear God, I ask that you remove from my
mind, my heart and my life all of the am *nots* that I
have allowed to hold me back.

Please erase from my mind the thought that I am *not*
good enough.

Please remove from my heart that I am *not* loved
enough.

Please untie from my life everything that I clutch that
supports the belief that I am *not* enough.

Today, dear God, I come to you humbly and reverently
asking that you untie, eliminate and erase all of the
*nots* that have invaded every aspect of my life.

For your mercy and your grace I am so grateful.

Let these words take on the presence of the Holy Spirit
to become living conditions in my life.

And So It Is!

## Prayer for Divine Correction

Dear God:

What I need from you today is mercy.

I humbly ask for you to have mercy on me!

Have mercy on me, not only for all of the unkind,
unloving things I have done, but for all of the
unkind, unloving things I have thought about doing.

Have mercy on me for all of the mean and nasty things
I have said about myself and others.

Have mercy on me for being intolerant and impatient
with myself and others.

Have mercy on me for being critical and judgmental of
myself and others.

Have mercy on me for allowing fear to cause me to act
impulsively, causing pain to myself and others.

Have mercy on me for being motivated by greed,
taking more than I need, then wasting it.

*What I need from you*

*today is mercy.*

Have mercy on me for not telling myself and others the
truth about what I feel and then being angry when I
am asked to do things that I am unwilling, not ready
or too tired to do.

Have mercy on me for not asking for what I need and
then being angry when I don't get it.

Have mercy on me for being ungrateful for all that I
have received.

Have mercy on me when I am comparing myself to
others and being angry at them for doing what I
have not done, for receiving what I have not asked
for.

Have mercy on me for taking out my anger and frustrations on those I love the most and then beating up
on myself for doing it.

Have mercy on me for being afraid of doing the wrong
thing in the wrong way and then blaming other
people for what I have not done.

Have mercy on me when I am being argumentative.

Have mercy on me when I am whining and

complaining to others about myself, or to myself
about others.

Today, God, I need your mercy!

I acknowledge that by myself I can do nothing! It is
only through the power of your mercy and grace
that my thoughts, words and actions will be changed.

For the change that is taking place within me right
now, I am so grateful.

And So It Is!

## God's Promise

Dear God:

You are my light and my salvation, please help me understand why I am afraid to be all that you have created me to be.

It is your great pleasure to give me all the good things of life, yet I am still unable to receive, to accept, to welcome your joy, your peace, your abundance as everyday occurrences in my life.

You promised me, God, that when my father, my mother, my friends, my lover, my children, turned their backs on me, you would be there to guide me, protect me, love me just as I am. Please help me understand what it is that I fear that keeps me from relying on you totally for everything.

You promised me, God, that you would not let the enemy gain control over me, that you would hide me in the shadow of your almighty power and lead me to a rock, a safe place.

You promised me, God, that you would open doors for me that no one could close, and that you would close doors that no one could open. You promised that you would prepare a table before me, even when others said it would be impossible.

Today, I am willing to understand why I have not relied on your promises.

Today, I am willing to stand in the shadow of your almighty presence, to understand what it is that I do, that I fear, that keeps me from living the life you have prepared for me.

Please bring the answers and revelations lovingly and gently, so that I will be able to dwell in the house of your joy, peace, mercy, grace and love, and realize the freedom that you have given to me. For this and all that you have done, I am so very grateful.

Let it be so!

And So It Is!

## The Perfect Love

I love you today, God.

I love you for all you are in me, all you are through me, all you do as me.

I love the realization that your grace is my strength.

I love the understanding that your truth is my power.

I love the knowledge that your wisdom is my guidance.

I love the truth that you are my source and supply.

I love the peace your presence brings.

I love the forgiveness your mercy brings.

I love the answers your truth brings.

I love the joy your love brings.

As I become aware and embrace all that you are as the essence of me,

I realize that I love you today, God, and I thank you for loving me back.

And So It Is!

## A Blessing for the Body
*(General or In Times of Physical Pain)*

Dear God:

Bless my body today!

Shower every part of me with the strength of your
love.

Fill every muscle, every tissue, every cell, every organ
and every system of my body with divine radiance
and health.

Bless my body today, God!

Bless every part of me with divine strength and
wholeness.

Eliminate the ravages of self-abuse and negligent
self-care.

Fill every part of me with divine light that will
restore divine order to every part of my body.

Bless my body today!

Strengthen my body today, God!

Strengthen my arms and legs.

Strengthen my hands and feet.

Strengthen my heart and all of the systems supported by it.

Let the healing power of your strength flow through me to correct and eliminate all imbalance, disease and disharmony.

Bless my body with strength today!

I now ask for and open myself to receive renewed wholeness, health and strength in every part of my body.

I now ask for and open myself to receive divine love, light and order in every part of my body.

I praise my body!

I love my body!

I give thanks for my body!

I know that my body is whole, healed and blessed!

I feel good!

My body feels good!

For this I am so grateful.

And So It Is!

## Prayer for a Married Couple

Dear God:

Bless my marriage today.

Bless me and my wife/husband with a clear vision of your purpose for our union.

Bless us by ordering our steps.

Bless our prayers for each other. Bless us with safety from all harm. Bless us with a peaceful and loving home. Bless us with hearts that are open and filled with gentle compassion for each other.

Bless us so that we will remember to compliment and encourage each other.

Bless us with strength from the inside that spills forth to the outside so that no weapon can be formed against us or within us.

Bless my wife/husband in everything that s/he does this day.

Bless her/his thoughts, words and deeds in every
situation and under all circumstances.

Bless and fill my wife's/husband's heart with
overwhelming peace and joy. Hear her/his every
concern and bring every appropriate solution to
her/his mind clearly and gently.

Bless me with patience so that I may be a more tolerant
partner.

Bless me to know and to see only the things that really
matter and to surrender all habits of thought or
speech that breed discord.

Bless our finances today. Remind us to use our
resources wisely and to give of our first fruits to you.

Bless us so that we will cooperate with each other.

Bless us so that we will see the goodness of your
presence in each other.

Bless us with kind thoughts of each other that spill
forth from our mouths as kind words.

Bless us to know when to speak up and when to listen.

Bless us to hear with our hearts, not our hurts.

Bless our marriage to be a breeding place for your
presence and your love.

Dear God, I invite you into the center of my marriage
so that it may grow to be all that you created it
to be.

For the blessings of your peaceful, loving presence in
the center of my marriage, I am so grateful.

Let it be so!

And So It Is!

# A Father's Prayer for His Child

Dear God:

Into thy hands I offer the mind, body and spirit of my son/daughter _____ *(state child's name),* asking that you raise him/her in the way you have created him/her to go. Guide my child away from all things and people that are not aligned with his/her highest good. Protect my child from those things and people that would lead him/her down a path that is not in alignment with his/her destiny as you have written it on his/her heart.

Remove from my child's mind all shadows of fear, doubt, anger and resentment that could cloud his/her mind or harden his/her heart.

Strengthen my child to walk away from those things

and people that can in any way keep him/her from the divine path that you have laid before him/her.

Open my child's eyes that he/she will see and know danger. Give my child the courage to resist all temptations that may lead to harm.

Teach _____ *(state child's name)* to honor his/her body as your divine temple.

Teach my child to cherish the power of his/her mind.

Teach my child to use his/her gifts and talents wisely.

Soften my child's heart with kindness and compassion.

Most of all, God, let my child know that you love him/her. Let my child feel your love, know your love and express your love at all times, under all circumstances.

Draw my child close to you. Drive my child away from patterns of thought and behavior that are not productive, honorable, healthy or self-loving.

Sprinkle my child liberally with your grace and light.

Teach my child your ways and guide him/her to make them a priority in life.

God, teach me to speak to my son/daughter in a way that honors his/her spirit and encourages him/her to desire to do good at all times.

Forgive me for the fears that I hold in my heart and project onto my child.

Remind me not to take my child for granted.

Teach me how to communicate and demonstrate my love in healthy and loving ways.

If there is anything that I do or say that does not set a good example for my child, please heal me of it right now!

In full faith and confidence, I ask that you create a bond of love, joy, harmony, respect and kindness between me and my son/daughter that cannot be broken by the ways of the world.

Thank you, God!

Thank you, God!

Thank you, God!

For I know that as I pray this prayer, thy will is done. Let it be so!

And So It Is!

# A Mother's Prayer for
# Her Child(ren)

Blessed and Divine Father God, Holy and Merciful Mother God:

Thank you for trusting me with the tasks and duties of being a mother. Thank you for the blessing that my child(ren) are in my life. Thank you for establishing a bond of love between me and my child(ren) that cannot be broken, that is life sustaining, that is whole and holy.

Thank you, God, for blessing my child(ren).

I pray that you will always bless their minds to be clear of all shadows of doubt. Bless their hearts to be kind. Bless their dreams that they may be fulfilled by your grace.

Thank you for sustaining my child(ren) through the difficult experiences they will face in this life.

Thank you for writing your will and your ways upon

their hearts and for calling them into remembrance in times of need.

I pray that you give them courage. Give them strength! Give them a mind and a heart to do what is good and peaceful.

Thank you, God, for loving my child(ren) even more than I do.

I pray that you love them when they feel hurt. Love them when they feel fear. Love them when they are not strong enough to love themselves.

Thank you, God, for protecting and guiding my child(ren) when I am not around.

I pray that every good thing I have done for them stays present in their minds and fills their hearts. That my words and deeds serve as good examples to them and for them.

Thank you for providing every need, fulfilling every dream and purifying every desire that my child(ren) may have.

Thank you, God, for not turning your eyes away from my child(ren).

Thank you for my child(ren)'s health and strength.

Thank you for lifting them above harm and steering them away from danger.

Thank you for the coating of loving light and protection that encircles them wherever they may be.

Thank you, God, for your promise that a mother's prayer for her children will never go unheard or unanswered.

For this I am so grateful.

And So It Is!

## A Mother's Prayer for Her Unborn Child

Blessed and Merciful God,

Thank you for the gift of life.

Thank you for the life of the child growing inside me.

Thank you for your love that is shaping and forming
this child's life into divine perfection.

Thank you for shaping this child's mind.

Thank you for shaping this child's bones.

Thank you for shaping this child's destiny and for
writing it upon his or her heart.

Thank you for filling this child's entire being with your
loving light.

Thank you for knowing and calling this child's name
even as it is being formed.

Thank you for showing me how to love this child even
before it is born.

*Thank you for the*

*gift of life.*

Thank you for giving me a healthy appetite for those
foods that are life giving and life sustaining while this
child is growing inside me.

Thank you for giving me peaceful rest while this child
is growing inside me.

Thank you for keeping me from harm and danger
while this child is growing inside me.

Thank you for peace of mind while this child is
growing inside me.

Right now I give to you all of my concerns for the
health, strength and well-being for the precious life
growing inside my body.

Right now I call forth your grace, mercy and the
loving light of your presence to fill my being and
sustain the life growing inside me.

Prepare me for this birth. Prepare my mind. Prepare
my body.

Bless me and this child that its birth will happen easily
and effortlessly, under the grace of your peace.

I give your angels charge of this child.

I give you charge over my entire being.
I give you thanksgiving and praise for this blessed life
　　growing inside me.
May this prayer be lifted, heard and accepted into the
　　highest realms of all that is good.
For this I am so grateful.
And So It Is!

## Prayer for Protection

Blessed Holy Spirit:

As I move into this day,

I claim the light of your protection for me and my
loved ones.

I claim the embrace of your protection around my
children.

No harm shall come near them.

I claim the embrace of your protection around my
wife/husband.

No harm shall come near her/him.

I claim the embrace of your protection around myself.

No harm shall come near me.

I claim the embrace of your protection around my
parents.

No harm shall come near them.

I claim the embrace of your protection around my
home.
No harm shall come near it.
I claim the embrace of your protection around my car
(or any mode of transportation).
No harm shall come near me.
Holy Spirit, keep us from all harm this day.
I know it is your will that we shall be protected in our
coming and going.
Let thy will be done.
And So It Is!

## A Prayer for Self-Forgiveness

Blessed and Divine Holy Spirit:

Please hear my words and shower me with grace. I now call upon you, Holy Spirit, for the presence of your mercy and your love. I ask that my guardians, angels, guides and all spirits of light surround me. Take these words that I speak into the bosom of your love, transforming them into something beautiful in my life that I can use to serve God and the world.

In cooperation with Spirit, I now forgive myself for
judging myself to be unacceptable.

In cooperation with Spirit, I now forgive myself for
judging myself to be not enough.

In cooperation with Spirit, I now forgive myself for
judging myself to be not good enough.

In cooperation with Spirit, I now forgive myself for
judging myself to be a problem to others.

In cooperation with Spirit, I now forgive myself for
    judging myself to be a burden to others.
In cooperation with Spirit, I now forgive myself for
    judging myself to be bad.
In cooperation with Spirit, I now forgive myself for
    judging myself to be unlovable.
In cooperation with Spirit, I now forgive myself for
    judging myself to be no good.
In cooperation with Spirit, I now forgive myself for
    judging myself to have something wrong with
    me.
In cooperation with Spirit, I now forgive myself for
    judging myself to be wrong.
In cooperation with Spirit, I now forgive myself for
    judging myself to be a victim.
In cooperation with Spirit, I now forgive myself for
    judging myself to have no value.
In cooperation with Spirit, I now forgive myself for
    judging myself to be unwanted.
In cooperation with Spirit, I now forgive myself for
    judging myself not to fit in my family.

In cooperation with Spirit, I now forgive myself for
    judging myself to always need to prove my worth.
In cooperation with Spirit, I now forgive myself for
    judging myself to be unworthy.
In cooperation with Spirit, I now forgive myself for
    judging myself to be anything less than a beloved
    child of God.
Through the power and grace of self-forgiveness, I now
    acknowledge and declare myself to be whole, holy,
    perfect and complete.
And So It Is!

## The Freedom of Forgiveness

Today, I ask for and claim forgiveness from everyone for
all ills I have created in thought, word or deed.

Today, all is forgiven. I am free to pursue my highest
good.

Today, I know no harm, no hurt, no condition, situation
or person is more powerful than the power of God
or God's love.

God's love protects me, provides for me and guides me.
All is well in my soul.

Today, I open my heart to the power of God's love. I
forgive. I am forgiving. I am forgiven.

Thank you, God.

And So It Is!

## Please Forgive Me

O Lord, please forgive me for indulging my human fantasies, weaknesses and fears! Please forgive me for affirming the things that I *do not* want or am *afraid to face.* Forgive me for engaging in the trivial, dancing with negativity and for acting as if I can do things that you and I both know are beyond the scope of my abilities.

Forgive me, Lord, for thinking too much, talking too much, for acting when I should be communing with you.

Forgive me for pushing, struggling and, in more ways than I can name, putting my agenda ahead of your will.

Forgive me for saying it is *them* causing strife when I know it is me.

Forgive me for looking out there when I need to look within.

Forgive me for saying one thing and doing another.

Forgive me for asking for things when I have not expressed gratitude for what I have.

Forgive me for attempting to do too many things at once, doing none of them well and then blaming you for all you have given me to do.

Forgive me for wallowing in my failures, second-guessing the truth and for generally being a human doing rather than a divine being.

Forgive me for judging myself, criticizing myself, doubting myself, and when that becomes too much to bear, turning on other people.

Forgive me for being human, not liking it and all the while asking you to give me more of the creature comforts that cause my stress in the first place.

Forgive me for believing that you are obligated to serve me when I have not always been willing to serve you.

Forgive me, God, because at this moment I am having a very difficult time forgiving myself.

I now ask for and open myself to receive your forgiveness and the peace and joy it brings to me. In the presence of your forgiveness, I am renewed, refreshed and reminded that you already know, even before I ask.

For this and so much more, I am so grateful.

And So It Is!

## Prayer for Strength When Doing Something New

Dear God:

Today, I am remembering that I am your child.

I know I am safe in the arms of your love.

I know I am protected by the power of your love.

I know I am guided by the wisdom of your love.

Today, I know I am a beloved child of God.

I know that all of my needs are met by God today.

I know that all of my questions are answered by God today.

I know that my concerns are God's concerns because I am God's Beloved child.

I am leaning on God today.

I am depending on God today.

I am putting my faith in God today.

I am putting my hand in God's today, so he can lead
me safely through whatever I fear.
I am trusting God with all the affairs of my life today
because I know God loves me just as I am, today and
every day.
For this I am so grateful.
And So It Is!

*I am a beloved*

*child of God.*

## Prayer for Peace in Difficult Tasks

Dear God:

Please remind me that I can do anything for a little while.

I can do repetitive chores.

I can do unpleasant things.

I can do difficult tasks, surrounded by difficult people, under the most unpleasant circumstances.

I can do all of the things that I have convinced myself that I am afraid to do.

Please remind me that I can do anything for a little while.

I can feel uncomfortable.

I can feel inadequate, unworthy or ill-equipped and still move forward in a positive direction until I feel better.

I can feel unsure.

I can feel my faith waning and my strength draining
and still accomplish something good, something
great, something worthwhile.

Please, God, remind me that I can do anything for a
little while.

When I feel like running away or turning around,
please remind me.

When I am making excuses and trying to find a way
out, please remind me.

When I am whining and complaining, please, God,
remind me that no task is too small, unimportant or
insignificant. Remind me that all I do for you today
will be rewarded tenfold tomorrow.

Please, God, remind me that I can do anything for a
little while. And while I am doing all that has been
given to me to do, remind me to give you praise for
the ability to do anything at all.

For the presence of your peace in the midst of all of
my duties, I am eternally and humbly grateful.

And So It Is!

## Prayer for the Overwhelmed

Dear God:

> I don't need to know how.
> I don't need to know when.
> I don't need to know why.
> I don't need to know where.
> All I need to know is *Who.*

Thank you for being the one *Who* is always there for me. The one *Who* never fails to respond to my frantic pleas for help.

Thank you for being the one *Who* is always dependable, ready and able to support, protect and guide me through the situations I face in my life.

Thank you for being the one *Who* knows the answer and offers it freely.

No matter where I am or what I may need, you are

always the one *Who* will take me by the hand and
pull me through.

Thank you for being the one *Who* knows me better
than I know myself. *Who* loves me when I can't find
love within myself. No matter what the situation or
experience, you, God, are *Who* I need and what I
need.

Thank you for being just *Who* you are and for
supporting me, guiding me, pushing me into being a
better me.

For who you inspire me to be, I am so grateful.

And So It Is!

## To Eliminate Tiredness
## or Exhaustion

Dear God:

I acknowledge you as the life and joy of living within me.

I acknowledge you as the indestructible, omnipresent substance of my life.

I acknowledge you as the perfecting harmony within all things.

I acknowledge you as the strength within me, through which I can do all things.

I now call forth the harmony that is God to be present in my mind.

I now call forth the joy that is God to be present in my heart.

I now call forth the strength that is God to be present in my body.

I now rest in the awareness that wherever I am, God is!
Where God is, all things are possible.
Thank you, God, that I am renewed in my mind, body and spirit.
Thank you, God, that I am rejuvenated in my mind, body and spirit.
Thank you, God, that I am refreshed in my mind, body and spirit.
Thank you, God, that I am revitalized in my mind, body and spirit.
Thank you!
Thank you!
Thank you!
And So It Is!

## To Speak the Truth

Beloved and Wise Holy Spirit:

Help me to say the most appropriate thing, in the most
loving way in my communication with _____
*(state person's name)*.

Clear my mind and heart of all past judgments, projec-
tions and prejudices.

Clear my mind and heart of all past anger, fear, hurt
and resentment.

Let me speak clearly, lovingly and honestly about what
is going on right now.

Let me speak with gentle compassion and kindness.

In speaking about _____ *(state situation)*
to _____ *(state person's name)*,
guide me to choose each word from the treasure
chest of your wisdom.

Open _____ *(state person's name)*
   mind, heart and ears to hear every word I speak in
   the spirit of genuine concern and compassion with
   which I offer it.

Open my mind, heart and ears to receive any feedback
   from _____ *(state person's name)*
   with a spirit of wisdom.

It is my intention that the words of my mouth and the
   meditations of my heart regarding this matter breed
   a more open, honest and loving relationship between
   myself and _____.

Thank you, Holy Spirit.

And So It Is!

## Prayer of Thanksgiving

Dear God:

Thank you for reminding me of how powerful
  I Am.

Thank you for showing me that I Am protected and
  guided and illumined by your divine presence in
  my being.

Thank you, God, for sheltering me in the storm, for
  making the crooked places straight, for making a
  way out of no way out.

Thank you for forgiving me when I was unable or unwilling to forgive myself.

Thank you, God, for your mercy, for your grace, for
  your goodness that endureth forever as the power in
  my spirit.

Thank you, God, for reminding me that your love is
the power that gives life to my soul.
Thank you, God, for the Being I Am.
And So It Is!

## Blessing for a Meal

Dear God:

Thank you for preparing this table before us.

Thank you for the bounty of the earth, which
nourishes our bodies.

Thank you for the abundance of your goodness, which
sustains our lives, strengthening us to serve you more
effectively.

Thank you for the hands that prepared this meal and
for the joy of being able to share it.

For all we have received and all that is yet to come,
God, we are thankful! We are grateful! We are
fulfilled!

And So It Is!

## Just a Bit of Thanks!

Dear God:

I am so grateful! I am so grateful! I am so grateful!

You have blessed me with vision.

What a gift!

It is a gift to see myself in divine light, peaceful abundance, total and complete well-being, and to know that through your grace, it is done to me as I believe.

I am so grateful that my eyes can behold the beauty of life and that these eyes do not limit the bounty of your glory!

I am so grateful that my spiritual eyes give power to my thoughts. All that I can see will be granted to me as I believe.

I am so grateful that in my mind I can create a vision for myself and my life.

I am so grateful that through the power of your grace,
the mercy of your love, the fruits of my faith take
shape according to divine order and become a reality
in my life.
What a blessed gift you have given me!
The gift of vision.
To see! To believe! To achieve!
To know! To behold!
For this I am so grateful.
And So It Is!

## Prosperity Prayer

Divine prosperity is my birthright.

I shall not want.

I am a child of divine heritage, born to inherit the
kingdom of all that is good.

All that is health, wealth, love, peace and joy has been
divinely ordained mine because of all that I Am.

My Father gives me breath that I may live and move in
his perfecting presence.

My Father is not limited. I Am not limited. I shall not
be limited.

My Mother fills the earth with the bountiful presence
of everything I could ever need.

My Mother is not limited. I Am not limited. I shall not
be limited.

I shall not want for any good thing.

I shall not be denied any good thing.

Hidden doors now open.

Invisible channels are now free.

Divine abundance and prosperity flow to me with God's perfect grace, in perfect ways.

I now live in the sacred place of the Most High, where there is an unlimited supply of bountiful resources and abundant treasures.

I shall not want! I shall not want! I shall not want!

Lack—Get back!

Debt—I do not fret!

Dis-ease—Not for me!

I Am healthy! I Am wealthy! I Am FREE!

I Am whole! I Am a divine loving, loved, loveable child of a loving, giving, abundant source.

*I shall not want!*

I acknowledge my good. I accept my good. I receive my good, right here and right now!

*Life* shall not deny me any good thing.

I now *forbid* my mind (knock 3 times on the center of

*I shall not want for*

*any good thing.*

your forehead) to entertain any fears of lack or
scarcity.

I absolutely forbid this mind to dignify nonsense!

It makes no sense to deny my birthright.

It is my Father's pleasure, my Mother's will, my Father's
business, my Mother's joy, that I shall inherit the
kingdom of good.

*God* is Good! And I accept good as mine!

I now lay claim to the kingdom at the core of my soul.

I Shall Not Want! I Shall Not Want! I Shall Not Want!

Let it be so. And So It Is!

Thank you, Father God. Thank you, Mother God.

Thank goodness I shall not want!

And So It Is!

## Prayer to Eliminate Debt

Blessed Holy Spirit and Angels of Abundance:
I now stand ready to reconcile my accounts.
I am willing to be held financially accountable and fiscally responsible for all of my resources.
I am now ready to eliminate lack and debt from my life.
I acknowledge that there is an abundance of good in the universe.
I now call my consciousness into alignment with the essence, energy and principles of universal abundance.
I am ready to release lack and debt from my life.
I confess that I have not always honored my financial resources, and I forgive myself.
I confess that I have not always honored my financial commitments, and I forgive myself.

I confess that I have not always honored my financial
responsibilities, and I forgive myself.

I confess that I have not always honored the principles
of money and finances, and I forgive myself.

I now surrender all thoughts of guilt, shame and fear
related to my past relationship with money, wealth,
abundance and prosperity.

I now open myself to a new understanding.

I now ask for and open myself to receive divine guidance that moves me out of debt.

I now ask for and open myself to receive divine in-
struction about the next most appropriate step I must
take toward financial responsibility.

I now ask for and open myself to receive divine inspiration about how best to use the financial resources
present in my life.

I now ask for and open myself to receive divine understanding of how to activate prosperity principles in
every aspect of my life.

I now ask for and open myself to receive the divine

and consistent flow of the abundance of the universe.

I now open my mind and my heart to the financial laws of the universe of divine good.

As I give, I receive!

As I say, I do!

As I ask, I am abundantly blessed!

For this I am so grateful.

And So It Is!

## Prayer of Gratitude

Dear God:

There is so much that I am grateful for today!

I have arms! I have legs! I have feet!

I can speak! I can think! I can hear! I can see!

I am well! My family is safe, and I am so grateful!

Today, I will allow gratitude to open new doors and
close old ones.

I will be grateful for everything! Every little thing!
Every big thing!

Today, I will allow gratitude to be my God!

Today, I will allow my grateful heart to let God know
that I am trusting, believing in and holding on to
God's promises.

I am grateful that God has promised that s/he will
clothe, feed and shelter me!

God has promised that s/he will open the sea, and that
   I will make it across without being drowned. God
   has promised that I shall not get weary! I shall not
   fall! I shall not be overcome by anything.
I am so grateful that God is with me; on my side and
   by my side!
What could possibly go wrong today?
*Nothing!* And for this, I am grateful.
And So It Is!

## I Am Thanking You
## Right Now

Dear God:

I want to thank you for what you have already done.

I am not going to wait until I see results or receive
   rewards, I am thanking you right now.

I am not going to wait until I feel better or things look
   better, I am thanking you right now.

I am not going to wait until people say they are sorry
   or until they stop talking about me, I am thanking
   you right now.

I am not going to wait until the pain in my body
   disappears, I am thanking you right now.

I am not going to wait until my financial situation
   improves, I am going to thank you right now.

I am not going to wait until the children are asleep and

the house is quiet, I am going to thank you right
now.

I am not going to wait until I get promoted at work or
until I get a new job, I am going to thank you right
now.

I am not going to wait until I understand every
experience in my life that has caused me pain or
grief, I am going to thank you right now.

I am not going to wait until the journey gets easier or
the challenges are removed, I am thanking you right
now.

I am thanking you because I am alive.

I am thanking you because I made it through the day's
difficulties.

I am thanking you because I have walked around the
obstacles.

I am thanking you because I have the ability and the
opportunity to do more and do better.

I am thanking you because you have not given up
on me.

I am thanking you because you have forgiven me.
I am thanking you because you love me and accept me
and acknowledge me when I cannot do it for myself.
I am not going to wait another moment or hour or day.
I am thanking you right now for every little thing you
have already done.
Thank you, God!
Thank you, God!
Thank you, God!
For all I have already received and all that is yet to
come!
And So It Is!

## Thank God for Faith!

Dear Father/Mother God:

Thank you for the gift of faith.

When I am alone and frightened, faith is there.

When it appears that my resources and reserves are diminished, faith is there.

When my friends shut their eyes and turn their backs, faith is there.

When I make decisions and choices that are not in my best interests, faith is there.

When my human world is in turmoil, faith is there.

When my human mind can no longer see the goodness you have in store for me, faith is there.

I am so grateful for the gift of faith.

I cannot buy it. I cannot borrow it. I need only to acknowledge you in all my ways and faith is there;

with its Mother, Grace, and its Father, Mercy, always
at my side.
I am faith-filled, I am faithful. I know your angels are
faithfully watching over me and paving my way.
Thank you, Father/Mother God.
For this I am so grateful.
And So It Is!

## Prayer for Faith

Dear God:

In every difficulty remind me that faith in you will stop the arrows of the adversary.

Remind me that faith in you can move mountains and people.

Remind me that, with faith in you, I gain strength and vision.

Remind me that, with faith in you, I may not know what you will do, but as long as I know what you can do, as long as I have faith that you will do your perfect will in the perfect way, I will be just fine.

Remind me to let faith in you be my guide, my protection, my shield and the light on my path.

Remind me that faith in you will bring me peace in the midst of the storm.

Faith will answer my questions.

Faith will open my path.

Faith will guide my thoughts.

Remind me that regardless of what appears, I can
always depend on you because you, God, are faithful.

And So It Is!

## The Divine Power in Me

There is a divine power seeking its expression in me, as
   me and through me.

The instrument of divine power is my mind.

Today, I believe in the divine power within me.

I believe the power is right where I Am.

I understand that this is a power of good and of God.

I realize the power flows through me at all times.

Today, I accept the presence of divine power within
   me.

Today, I believe the power is operating in all of my life's
   affairs.

Today, I acknowledge that there is a divine power
   instructing me in all that I do.

Today, I affirm divine power as the active presence of
   joy and happiness in my life.

Today, I deliberately turn from everything and everyone
that denies the reality of divine power in me, as me
and through me.

Today, I know that every atom, every cell, every tissue,
every organ in my body is brought into divine health
and harmony.

Today, I know every shadow of doubt, worry and fear is
dispelled as I Am quickened with the divine power
of the living spirit in me.

Today, I Am graced with the presence of divine power.

Today, I Am blessed with the love of divine power.

Today, I Am strong in the glory of divine power.

Today, I know I Am the instrument through which the
divine power is working.

Today, I affirm that the divine power within me now
breathes newness into my being and every aspect of
my life.

I Am filled with good. I Am filled with light. I Am
filled with faith. I Am filled with the truth of my
being, which is enduring, dynamic and divine.

*I am filled with good. I am filled with*

*light. I am filled with faith.*

Thank You, Spirit! Thank You, Spirit! Thank You,
   Spirit!
Let it be so!
And So It Is!

## In Fear or Anxiety

Dear God:

Today, I open my heart and make myself available to
experience and express the fullness of your presence.

In your presence I know that my strength is renewed.

In your presence I know peace, joy, harmony and
balance.

In your presence I see myself and all others from a new
place, with eyes of love and acceptance.

In your presence, in every situation and under all
circumstances, I am surrounded by power, glory and
victory.

In your presence old patterns of thought, behavior,
action and reaction fall away and are replaced by a
positive momentum toward the experience of all
things good.

In your presence all feelings of panic, anxiety, distress,

imbalance, frustration and fear disappear instantly. My heart is opened and cleansed of all toxic emotions. My mind is free of all wayward thoughts that promote anger, judgment or disharmony within and without.

In your presence the truth wells up within me. The truth rises up my spine. The truth penetrates my mind. The truth fills my heart. The truth is, I cannot be overwhelmed, overtaken, overshadowed, overrun or overlooked in the presence of God.

Today, through the presence of God within me, I experience *all that God is* rising up from the root, the core, the essence of my being.

Today, through the presence of God within me, I express the fullness of God's glory, which makes all things new.

Oh, what a joyful experience it is to know that you, God, are on my side! To know that God's presence is the truth of my being.

For this I am so grateful.

And So It Is!

## In Times of Despair

Blessed Holy Spirit:

I need to feel your comfort.

I need to feel your strength.

I need to feel your peace.

I need to feel your joy.

I need to know that I am surrounded by your divine
light and love.

I now ask for and open myself to receive a full
outpouring of your presence.

In and to your presence I surrender every thought,
belief, judgment, perception and feeling that supports
the experience of loneliness, confusion, desperation
and pain.

I embrace your presence, Holy Spirit, and I now claim
relief!

I now claim peace!

I now claim joy!
With a grateful heart I say,
Thank You, Holy Spirit!
Thank You, Holy Spirit!
Thank You, Holy Spirit!
And So It Is!

## In Regret

Dear God:

Please help me live in this right-now moment. Show
me how to stop running from the past and hiding
from the future.

Help me to be present with the goodness, the joy, the
beauty, the peace that is available to me right here,
right now.

Let me know that I no longer need to beat myself up
for things I did not do or did not complete.

When I start judging myself for how dumb I've been,
all the stupid mistakes I've made and the behavior
patterns that have caused so much pain in my life,
*stop me!*

When I am reminding myself that I'm not good
enough, smart enough or ready to move forward,
*please change my mind!*

When I am giving myself excuses and using delaying
tactics that keep me from taking the next step, move
me forward, in spite of myself.

Help me to stop running, waiting and hiding.

Help me to remember that everything I need is present
right where I am in this moment.

Help me to use my past as a stepping stone into the
goodness of right now.

Help me to let go of the things that are dragging me
down and pushing me back.

Help me to see beyond the obstacles and challenges
that I imagine to be blocking my way.

Help me to relax, to surrender, to step into the peace
that is here *right now!*

Let me feel the peace of your presence and the power
of your love, right now.

Help me move into this moment without any fear
of what it holds or anxiety about what lies
beyond.

God, I need you right now!

I know that every word I have spoken has reached a
   special place in your heart.
For this I am so grateful.
And So It Is!

*(Spend the next few moments in silence.)*

## In Times of Loneliness

Blessed and Divine Holy Spirit:
I now ask that you fill my heart with love.
I am standing in a place of loneliness and despair.
I am experiencing confusion and conflict.
I am feeling lost and abandoned.
Please fill my heart with the joy of your love.
There is a battle going on inside of me.
I am battling loneliness.
I am battling self-doubt.
The battle is becoming difficult.
It feels like I am losing my joy, my peace and my self.
Holy Spirit, please fill me with the strength of your
    love.
Fill my heart with the power of your love.
Fill my heart with the presence of your love.

I now open my heart.
I now open my mind.
I now open my life to the love of the Holy Spirit.
And So It Is!

## In Times of Grief

Dear God:

You promised me that your comfort would come to me
in times of despair.

You promised me that if I would lean on you and call
on you, I would find peace.

I come to you now filled with grief and despair at the
loss of _____ *(state the name
of the person or the situation).*

I am leaning on you for strength.

I am calling on you for understanding.

I am reaching out to you for comfort.

I am depending on you to help me learn how to accept
this loss.

Help me, Holy Spirit.

Guide me, Holy Spirit.

*Help me, Holy Spirit. Guide me, Holy*

*Spirit. Comfort me, Holy Spirit.*

Comfort me, Holy Spirit.

Give me peace. Give me peace. Give me peace.

Leaning on the promises of God, through the power
and presence of the Holy Spirit, I am now filled
with comfort and peace.

And So It Is!

## For Wisdom Through Grief

Dear God, Blessed and Divine Holy Spirit:

I acknowledge you as the knower of all things.

I acknowledge you as the director of the process of life
and living.

I acknowledge you as being at the center of all things.

I acknowledge you as the beginning and the end.

I acknowledge that at this moment my heart is filled
with grief at the loss of _____ *(state
the name of the person or the situation).*

I now ask for and open myself to receive divine understanding of how to accept this loss.

I now ask for and open myself to receive divine
guidance in how to walk through this experience
with grace and ease.

I now ask for and open myself to receive divine

revelations of how to use the experience of this loss
for my own personal growth and healing.

I now ask for and open myself to the courage to do
whatever I am called upon to do.

I now surrender all of the "whys" to you.

I now call forth the peace-filled, comforting presence
and power of the spirit of God.

Unto you, dear God, I surrender this grief.

Fill me with peace.

Fill me with comfort.

Fill me with acceptance.

Fill me with strength.

Fill me with courage.

I now declare it to be so.

And So It Is!

## When You've Been Hurt

Dear God:

*Create in me a clean heart, renew a right spirit within me.*

I have been so angry for so long, with so many people,
    including myself.

*Create in me a clean heart, renew a right spirit within me.*

I have withheld my love, my support, even my
    gratitude from those who have been the most
    supportive to me.

*Create in me a clean heart, renew a right spirit within me.*

I have lashed out at those who mean the most to me.

*Create in me a clean heart, renew a right spirit within me.*

I have behaved in inappropriate ways for all of the
    wrong reasons.

*Create in me a clean heart, renew a right spirit within me.*

I have dishonored myself and disrespected others who
    did not deserve it.

*Create in me a clean heart, renew a right spirit within me.*
I have allowed fear and anger, shame and guilt, unwor-
thiness and doubt to control my thoughts and direct
my actions.
*Create in me a clean heart, renew a right spirit within me.*
I have allowed my disappointment in people to become
my disappointment with you.
*Create in me a clean heart, renew a right spirit within me.*
I have allowed resentment to breed in my heart, which
has led me to distrust you.
*Create in me a clean heart, renew a right spirit within me.*
I have allowed habits to rule me, disobedience to
control me and a lack of discipline to take me away
from the purpose you have placed in my heart.
*Create in me a clean heart, renew a right spirit within me.*
I have not been honest with myself and others.
*Create in me a clean heart, renew a right spirit within me.*
I have been hurtful without cause, and as a result, my
heart is heavy.
*Create in me a clean heart, renew a right spirit within me.*

I now surrender to you everything within me that is
   not of you.
It is my deepest desire to serve you and to offer to
   myself and others all of the love and compassion you
   have shown to me.
To know that you are the truth within me, I ask that
   you
*Create in me a clean heart, dear God, and renew a right
   spirit within me.*
For all I have received and all that is yet to come,
I am eternally grateful.
And So It Is!

## Prayer When Ending
## a Relationship
*(or in Any Experience of Sudden Loss)*

Dear God:

Today, I ask for the strength to let go. I know that this experience has served its purpose in my life. I know that the time has come to move forward, but I am afraid. Please give me the strength to let go.

Today, I ask for the courage to move forward. I know that there is no more I can give, nothing else I can receive, by remaining where I am. I know that your divine purpose has been served and that there is something even greater waiting for me on the other side of this, but right now I am in pain. The pain that I feel keeps me stuck right where I am. Please give me the strength and the courage to move forward.

Today, I ask for the wisdom to forgive. I feel so much anger. So much shame. So much guilt. I am trying so hard to figure out what I did, what I should have done, what I should have stopped doing long before now. I know that if I could forgive myself and everyone else involved, I would be able to see beyond this experience. I would be able to move beyond this anger and grief, but right now I am angry. I know it is this anger that keeps me right here and feeling this way. Please give me the strength, courage and wisdom to forgive myself; then I know I will be able to forgive everyone else.

Today, I ask for understanding. I am trying to understand, but the truth is, I don't! I am trying to see the good in this, but the truth is, I can't see it! I am trying to make sense of what is going on so that I will not continue to feel the anger or the fear. If for some reason it is not time for me to understand, please, God, just take away the pain.

Today, I ask for the humility of acceptance. I confess that I do not like what is going on. I do not understand why this is happening. I am willing to humble myself. I am willing to accept this experience, but right now I want to fight. Please humble my spirit so that I may move toward acceptance.

Today, I ask for peace. I cry out for peace! I know that the presence of peace surpasses understanding. I now ask for the comforting presence of peace to overtake the fear and anger that threaten to consume me. I know that with peace I will grow in strength and courage, and I will find myself in the midst of this loss. I now open myself to receive and experience peace in the midst of this storm. I now anchor my soul in the presence of peace. I now receive and embrace the presence of peace as the reality of this moment.

Today, I stand with strength! I move with courage! I act wisely! I am open to divine understanding! I humbly accept all of my thoughts and feelings, and I experience the presence of total peace.

For this and so much more, I am so eternally grateful. And So It Is!

## In My Weakest Moment

The place on which I am standing right now is Holy
  Ground.
I am standing in the midst of my own personal spiritual
  transformation, and it is unfolding perfectly.
In the midst of my most difficult lesson, I am gaining
  strength, growing in power, increasing in wisdom
  and being fulfilled in every need.
In my weakest moment, I am faced with a divine
  opportunity for God to demonstrate just how awe-
  some the power of God is in me.
I know this to be true.
I accept this to be true.
Right now, right where I am, the experience and ex-
  pression of the truth I need to know is manifesting
  perfectly.
What a blessing! And So It Is!

## Prayer of Surrender

Dear God:

Today, I acknowledge, accept and admit that my life is a God-job, and I surrender my life to you.

Today, I surrender fear, doubt, worry, anxiety and control.

Today, I acknowledge, accept and admit that I cannot fix anyone or anything.

Today, I acknowledge, accept and admit that I cannot change anyone or anything.

Today, I acknowledge, accept and admit that I cannot heal anyone or anything.

Today, I acknowledge, accept and admit that I cannot help anyone.

Today, I acknowledge, accept and admit that I cannot control anyone or anything.

*I surrender my*

*life to you.*

Today, I acknowledge, accept and admit that I cannot fix, change, heal or help myself.

I am a God-job. My life is a God-job.

Today, dear God, please work on me, in me, through me. Work on my life, my relationships, all of my affairs, on everyone and everything in my life.

Today, dear God, please have your perfect way with me, for I know that the least you can be to me and for me is good.

For this I am so grateful.

And So It Is!

## Prayer for Healing

Dear God:

Today, I claim healing of anything that stands between you, me and total well-being in my life.

Today, I claim the healing power, healing presence, healing light, healing love of the loving Universal Mind as my divine right.

Today, I claim healing in all of my affairs, relations and relationships!

I claim healing in my conscious and subconscious mind.

I claim healing in my total being!

I claim healing of the past!

I claim healing for the future!

I claim healing for my finances!

I claim healing for my loved ones!

I now claim that no harm can come near me, my

dwelling or those I hold near and dear in my heart!
I now acknowledge, I accept and I acclaim that I, by
myself, can do nothing.
I now know, I now affirm, I now claim that the healing
power of life, of light and of love is showering down
on me right now.
All is well in my mind, my body, my spirit and my life.
For this I am so grateful.
And So It Is!

## Prayer for Peace

Today, I need to be still and let God love me.

God's love is my strength.

God's love is my protection.

God's love is my light in the midst of any darkness.

God's love is the fulfillment of every hunger, every thirst.

God's love is my source and my supply.

God's love, ever present, is the only thing I need, want or seek today.

For in the presence of God's love, all is well in my life and in my soul.

Today, I need to be still and let God love me.

As I speak these words, as I think these words, they take on the presence of the Holy Spirit to become the circumstances of this day in my life.

Let it be so. And So It Is!

## The Power of Peace

Today, I decree there is but one power and one
   presence operating in my mind, my body, my life and
   all of my affairs.
I decree that the presence and the power of peace
   consumes me.
I shall decree a thing, and it shall be established unto me.
The melody of peace now sings in my soul.
I now dance the dance of peaceful freedom.
I now radiate the love and peace of the divine.
I now draw from every experience the highest and the
   best.
I Am confident, peace filled and spiritually powerful.
There is a Lily in the Valley, and all is well in my soul.
I now decree it so.
And So It Is!

*The melody of peace now*

*sings in my soul.*

## Prayer for World Peace

Precious Lord of the Universe:

Today, *I am* laying down all weapons of anger and
attack in my thoughts, my words and my actions.

Today, *I am* laying down the grievances and upsets that
have led me to attack others and brutally assault
myself.

Today, *I am* laying down all thoughts of criticism and
judgment, all words of destructive defensiveness and
all acts of vicious vengeance and violence against
myself and all others.

Today, I ask that you cleanse me of all thoughts and
words of aggression, so that I may take the necessary
steps toward being peaceful in my own heart and
offering that peace to the world.

Today, I ask that you remind me how important *I am* in
ensuring the active presence of peace.

Today, *I am* opening my heart and sending forth the
   light of love to all world leaders.
Today, *I am* opening my mind to the creation and
   experience of a world where aggression and violence
   sleep forever.
Today, *I am* opening my eyes to be aware of everything
   I can do or say that will promote the presence of
   peace.
Today, I realize that peace begins with me.
Today, I humbly surrender myself, every thought I
   think, every word I speak, everything I do, to the
   creation, maintenance and advancement of peace.
Today, I ask for peace, I invite peace in and I dedicate
   myself to promoting peace in my every experience.
Let the light of peace reign in me!
May the presence of peace reign in the world.
Let the power of peace shine forth through me!
May peace pervade the world!
Let it be so!
And So It Is!

## Prayer of Celebration

This is the day that the Lord has said, "Rejoice!" I will rejoice and be glad for this day!

Am I enjoying this day? Have I given thanks for this day? Isn't it wonderful that when the Creator has a plan for me, and I am not, for whatever reason, on the path, situations will happen in my life to put me on the path? Life is about the *experience* of living! For this I am so grateful.

I know that wherever I am today I will be blessed! This is a divine opportunity to awaken to a little more of my God-ness. This is a perfect day to celebrate myself and the presence of God-ness within me. This is the only day I have in which to do what brings me joy.

I am not the same person I was yesterday, so if I will just take my eyes off of yesterday's challenges, God just might do something a little different for me today!

*I must rejoice and be*

*glad for this day!*

This is the day that God has made just for me to walk a little closer to God! This is the day that God has made just to show me what the presence of God will do for me if I will simply get out of God's way!

I think I'll go out and do something good for myself this day. Something fun! For that, God will applaud me. God will honor my desires. God will support me. God will love me, and I will be able to feel it. The only thing required of me is to be grateful.

Let it be so!

And So It Is!

## Evening Prayer

Good night, God.

I thank you for all I have experienced today.

I thank you for guiding me, protecting me, teaching me
   and keeping me safe from harm this day.

I thank you for every meal I have eaten today.

I thank you for protecting my family today.

I thank you for every kind word spoken to me and
   about me today.

I thank you for every opportunity I had today to help
   somebody, to listen to somebody, to remind
   somebody that each day is a blessing.

I thank you for forgiving me for every time I was
   intolerant or impatient today.

I thank you for your grace, your compassion, your
   generous and unconditional love.

As this day comes to a close, I ask for peaceful rest.
I ask that you renew my mind and your strength
within me.
I ask you to give me clear direction for tomorrow so
that I may know you better and serve you in a
greater way.
May the words of my mouth and the meditations of
my heart be acceptable to you this day and
forevermore.
And So It Is!

cm 11 13